Mike Pence

Mike Pence is ready to cooperate with the committee that's "going after Trump."

Former US Vice President Mike Pence continued his "opposition" directions to former President Donald Trump with a new statement that could hint at a future Republican contest between the two men. Former Vice President Mike Pence said on Wednesday that he would consider testifying before the House Committee "6 January" if requested, which Trump does not recognize, because it investigates his involvement in the riots by his supporters on Capitol Hill.

According to ABC, Pence said: "If there is an invitation to participate, I will take it into account."

This is Pence's first clear statement against Trump since the recent start of the FBI investigations into the former US president. Pence's answer was a new "clash" with his former chairman, Donald Trump, who repeatedly criticized the work of the 6 January committee as politically motivated. According to ABC, for months, the Commission's investigators have been communicating in particular with Pence's lawyers about securing his testimony in the incidents of the Capitol break-in. The former US president, Donald Trump, recently took care to defend himself when he received criticism for finding classified documents inside his Florida residence, saying he removed them from the "classification" before leaving the White House in January 2021, indicating that he had not broken the law.

On August 8, FBI agents called them at Trump's home in the Palm Beach area, searching for classified documents that Trump allegedly took from Washington, D.C., and did not respond to several repeated requests for their return.

Meet Vice President Trump's Mike Pence

Mike Pence is an American politician and governor of Indiana, whose choice as deputy presidential candidate Donald Trump in his race to the White House sparked controversy in America, in a move counted by trackers as Trump's inevitably difficult choice in his search for the support of Republican "evangelical" conservatives. Trump's election campaign was successful, with the GOP candidate winning the 2016 presidential election after a strong contest with Democratic nominee Hillary Clinton, to make Mike Pence the US vice president.

Generator and Genesis

Mike Pence was born on June 7, 1957 in Columbus, Indiana, to parents of Irish descent, and is married with three sons.

Study and Composition

Mike Pence pursued his high school studies in Columbus, earning a degree in history from Hanover College in 1981, and a doctorate in law in 1886 from the Indiana University School of Law Robert McKinney.

Intellectual orientation

Mike Pence defines himself as a conservative Christian and Republican, and has not hesitated to endorse the "Tea Party" movement, as he has become famous for his hardline positions on a number of social issues, such as abortion, which he has passed a law restricted by a federal court challenge. Republican presidential candidate Donald Trump describes him as a man who served with "excellence" in Congress and has "the skills of a very talented executive."

He asserts his support for Trump's rhetoric and directions, saying he was "someone who recognized the frustrations of ordinary Americans in a way that reminds us of former US President Ronald Reagan" He is a hero for many Republicans, adding that Trump "He will be a strong leader who will stand next to America's allies and destroy our enemies of freedom." "Together we will make history, together we will restore the American dream, it is time for that, together we will restore America's greatness again."

Functions and responsibilities

After graduating as a lawyer, Mike Pence then headed a 1991 research institution on Indiana's (conservative-oriented) policy, then became a member of the state's policy network, and since 1994 has been presenting state radio and television programmes between 1995 and 1999.

Political experience

Mike Pence entered politics, but failed to run for a congressional seat between 1988 and 1990, and was subsequently elected to Congress in November 2000, re-elected to other states for 12 years, and elected between 2009 and 2011 president of the Republican Party Convention. Between 2005 and 2007, Mike Pence led the Republican Conservative Group's "Republican Study Committee", subsequently serving as Governor of Indiana since 2013, and there was talk earlier that he could be nominated to contest the country's presidency in 2008 and 2012.

Pence disagrees with Trump in some positions, previously calling Trump's proposal to ban Muslims from entering the United States "aggressive and unconstitutional," as he declared his support for trade deals opposed by Trump.

Mike Pence also sparked controversy after the 2015 enactment of the Freedom of Religions Act, which allows business owners in Indiana not to engage in or participate in gay marriages based on their religious convictions, which was considered "discriminatory" by defenders of homosexual rights, and in 2009 his opposition to the Act on the Automatic Granting of American Citizenship to Children Born on American Soil. Mike Pence was a supporter of former President George Bush Jr. waging war on Iraq in 2003, opposed U.S. President Barack Obama's proposals to close the Guantánamo detention facility, and called for "enemy fighters" of the United States to be brought before military courts. Pence stated his support for Israel's right to "attack targets" of Iran to prevent it from "developing nuclear weapons", and also defended its use of "excessive force" in its war on the Gaza Strip, as well as the intervention of the Atlantic Treaty Forces (NATO) to overthrow Colonel Muammar Gaddafi in Libya.

Immediately after his appointment as the Republican Vice-Chancellor during the election race, Pence said that "Donald Trump recognizes the hopes of the American people and their future as no leader has realized them since Ronald Reagen."

"Americans can choose a leader who will strive to make America safe and prosperous again and bring about real change, or we can elect someone who literally embodies the failed establishment in Washington D.C. (D.C.)."

Following the appearance of Trump and Pence together, the Clinton campaign issued a statement saying that Pence was "the most extreme choice of this generation" and would "double down on Trump's divisive rhetoric and policies."

After the U.S. presidential election was held on November 8, 2016, Donald Trump became the 45th President of the United States of America, after winning by 276 votes against rival Hillary Clinton.

Mike Pence took over as vice president to help Trump lead the White House.

Trump: Former US president pressured Vice President Pence in "illegal" bid to overturn election results

A congressional commission of inquiry says former U.S. President Donald Trump put his vice president, Mike Pence, at risk during the Capitol riots, when he illegally pressured him to overturn the 2020 election.

Lawmakers heard this from Pence aides who explained the White House's efforts to reject President Joe Biden's victory.

Committee Chairman Benny Thompson said American democracy "resisted Trump's scheme" because the former vice president refused to submit to it. The committee accused Trump of attempting a coup d'état to stay in power. Trump supporters broke into the congressional building on January 6, 2021 in an effort to thwart Biden's victory testimony.

At the third plenary hearing, the Democratic-led committee focused on the constitutional process through which chairpersons are elected. Trump publicly made the claim, which he saw as both legal scholars and Pence's aides, saying vice presidents had the power to stop congressional certification of the election results. Greg Jacob, then Pence's adviser, testified that "the revision of the text, history and common sense frankly" confirmed that his boss had no authority to overturn the election results.

There had been none of America's founding fathers in the eighteenth century "to put one person, especially one who had a direct interest in the outcome, in a role that had a decisive impact on the results of the elections".

Michael Lutg, a conservative former judge and unofficial aide to Pence, said if the vice president had followed Trump's orders "America could have been plunged into what I think would have been a revolution in America's constitutional crisis." The hearing opened with footage of Capitol demonstrators shouting "hang for Mike Pence." in a speech outside the White House to do "the right thing."

At previous hearings, the Committee said that aides who were with Trump during the riots heard President Trump react in agreement, saying "he deserves it", after seeing television footage of his supporters chanting threats against Pence. Lawmakers on the committee argued that Trump continued his lobbying campaign, by tweeting that Pence had "no courage" to intervene, even after he knew that rioters had broken into the capitol.

"Mike Pence said no. He resisted pressure. He knew it was illegal. he knew it was a mistake ".

"This courage has put him in tremendous danger."

Pence was inside a congressional hall while rioters stormed the building

Mike Pence: Who is he and how did he move from Indiana to the White House?

US Vice President Mike Pence has become one of the most influential figures on the new White House administration team during Donald Trump's presidency. Who is it?

Over the past four years, Pence has been an efficient and skilled Vice-President, particularly in his leadership of the Panel, which decides on key appointments in the United States Administration, and in his presence before the media, where he praised his communication capabilities and his seamless delivery of his ideas. Pence was keen to work in the shadows, avoiding being present in the headlines of a lot of news; Although he recently came under the spotlight for his role in leading the White House coronavirus task force.

In a less prominent role, Pence was given responsibility for the United States space policy dossier with President Trump's reestablished National Space Council after having previously dissolved. Pence's trip to the White House began in July 2016, when Trump and his family met at his home in Indianapolis, where he was asked. Joining his team

It is easy to guess why Trump asked him to do so, because the former governor had the privilege of being socially conservative and was one who built a lot of experience in Washington (through his work in the House of Representatives).

Before Trump called him his choice for vice president, Pence publicly criticized Trump's policies.

He called Trump's proposal to ban Muslims from entering the United States "aggressive and unconstitutional", and also called his remarks about Judge Gonzalo Kuriel "inappropriate."

The business mogul had pointed out that the Mexican judge's legacy prevented him from delivering a fair trial in the case against Trump University.

However, Pence is now the second in the Trump administration and rarely criticizes the president.

There have been some bumps in Pence's way over the last four years.

Pence's first negative headlines were in 2017, and related to his use of his personal email while governor of Indiana.

He was accused of hypocrisy after harshly criticizing Hillary Clinton for the unusual arrangements in her use of her personal email, although he was not the same as her, and did not deal with confidential information on his own e-mail account at the Internet company "AoL", formerly known as "American Online."

He caused controversy when he announced in May that he would be happy to see Michael Flynn return to work in the Department. Flynn is the former national security adviser who resigned during the investigation into Russia's interference in the 2016 election with him.He also criticized Pence for his statements about the coronavirus in the United States, including his saying that panic about the virus outbreak was "exaggerated."

He told the Indiana Paul Star in 2012 that the two liberal characters: John F. Kennedy and Martin Luther King, inspired him at the beginning of his political career. The governor of Indiana, who describes himself as a "Christian, conservative and Republican, according to this sequence", voted for the Democratic presidential candidate, Jimmy Carter, in 1980. He explained that he remained so until his meeting at the Angelic Church of Karen, who later became his wife, where his views began to change. Pence served as governor of Indiana from 2013 to 2017, and also has 12 years of legislative work as a member of the U.S. House of Representatives. During his last two years in Washington, he served as president of the Republican House of Representatives' Caucus, the third highest leadership position in the Republican Party. He also chaired the Republican Studies Committee, a conservative Republican caucus, which, in some's view, gave him potential support from some evangelicals within the Republican Party.

Pence has previously contemplated running for the White House, and in 2009 he visited states with congresses and primaries to count presidential candidates, sparking speculation that he had ambitions to run for president in 2012. On the campaign trail in 2016, Pence was busy siding with Trump in a crowded campaign platform, appearing with him at several election rallies across the country - and usually traveling with him in a number of states daily. One of his key roles was to support the presidential candidate when some controversial issues arose: he defended Trump when he appeared to call people to arms against rival Hillary Clinton, and he stood up for his son, Donald Trump Jr., when he made remarks that likened refugees to "Skittles"; When he said, "If I had a bowl of Skittles candy, and I told you that only three of them would kill you, would you take a handful of them? This is our Syrian refugee problem ".

However, he disputed Trump's long-held view that former President Barack Obama was not born in the United States (days later, Trump himself said he had also changed his mind on the matter).

controversy

While Governor, Pence caused mass outrage when he signed the Religious Freedom (Restoration) Act. His critics accused the law of discriminating against the LGBT community (LGBT), by allowing businesses to refuse to provide services based on religious beliefs. Subsequently, under pressure from protests that spread at the national (federal) level, there was an amendment indicating that companies must not discriminate against LGBT people. This time, it drew criticism from conservatives who felt betrayed by signing the amendment. Pence was also known for his strong opposition to abortion.

Pence, an evangelical Christian and father of three, also when he was Governor of the State, signed into law one of the country's most stringent abortion laws. The State of Indiana had applied a ban on abortion based on the determination of the foetus's sex, race or diagnosis of a disability, and the law had subsequently been invalidated by a ruling of the Court of Appeal. In 2017, Pence became the first continuous vice president in the service to attend the "March for Life", the largest American gathering against abortion. He continued to attend this activity regularly. In 2012, Pence likened the Supreme Court's decision to uphold the Facilitated Health Care Act (known as the Obamacare Act) to attacks 11 September, in a closed-door meeting of Republican deputies. He later apologized for this analogy.

Pence warns that China is on track to become an "empire of evil"

Former US Vice President Mike Pence warned on Wednesday that China was on track to become a "empire of evil" that posed a greater risk to the US than the Soviet Union in the Cold War era. Former Vice President Donald Trump, who is believed to be considering running for president in the 2024 election, called on incumbent President Joe Biden to take on China more aggressively on several fronts. Including the source of the coronavirus and the "new colonization" of the Asian giant. "The Chinese Communist Party poses the greatest threat to our prosperity, security and values on Earth," Pence said, speaking at the Heritage Foundation. He added, "China may not be an empire of evil but it works hard every day to become so", noting that "communist China and in many respects, poses a greater challenge to the United States than the Soviet Union did during the cold war."

Trump and Pence have taken an anti-China stance against US economic competition, including imposing tariffs and holding Beijing responsible for the spread of the coronavirus. Trump has repeatedly seen President Xi Jinping, in the early days of the pandemic for China's transparency and professionalism in its public health response, before turning to criticism of Beijing and calling the coronavirus Pence said that instead of "crawling" into China, the Biden administration should demand Beijing "The source of the coronavirus revealed," reiterating Trump's statement that evidence suggests the coronavirus has leaked from the Wuhan lab.

Biden in May opened an investigation into Covid-19 sources. Pence said he believed China was "feeling weak in this new administration," and called on Biden to take further steps against Beijing.

He urged the president to "separate" the US economy from China in industries deemed essential to national security, strengthen economic relations with Taiwan, reduce Chinese imports and demand the transfer of the 2022 Winter Olympics from Beijing unless it provides real data on the origin of Covid-19 and ceases to persecute the Uighur Muslim minority.

He also called for a bold US stance to prevent China from building a military base in the western hemisphere. "The President must make it clear that the hemisphere is prohibited from China's new colonization," Pence said.

Former Vice President Donald Trump, Republican Mike Pence, who is likely to run for the next presidential election in 2024 in the United States, intends to publish the first part of his CV in 2023, the publishing house Samen & Chaster announced Wednesday. "I am grateful that I was able to present my life story to serve Americans, from Congress to Governor of Indiana, and then Vice President of the United States" between 2017 and 2021, the former radio presenter who studied rights wrote in a statement. A publishing house official said in the same statement that his "revealing biography will be close between the work on one of the most important presidential states in American history."

Mike Pence will talk about his life, his work and his "experience as a Christian", as well as the "many critical moments of the Trump administration," according to the publishing house, which explained that it had signed a contract for two Pence books.

She added: "The first book is currently scheduled to be published in 2023."

CN stated that the contract's value was between $3 million and $4 million.

With less than 10 days to go, calls for impeachment for the losing U.S. president, Donald Trump, are mounting, highlighting his vice president, Mike Pence, who could play a crucial role in accelerating Trump's removal from office and finally eliminating any hopes he may have of running again for office.

In this regard, CNN quoted a source close to Pence as saying that the latter did not exclude the possibility of applying the 25 amendment to the US Constitution, explaining that he would prefer to keep this option to resort to if Trump became less mentally balanced. The 25 amendments allow Pence and a majority of the government to declare the president ineligible to rule, becoming the acting president of the United States. House Speaker Nancy Pelosi said on Thursday that the House would not have to initiate impeachment proceedings if Pence, along with members of the government, disqualified Trump.

In addition, CNN reported that Pence's team had concerns about the application of the 25 amendment and Trump's impeachment, linked to the latter's possible exit and reckless steps that would put the entire United States at risk.

US news network sources indicated that Pence and Trump had not spoken until Saturday evening since supporters of the latter stormed the Capitol in a desperate attempt to prevent congressional ratification of Joe Biden's presidential election.

Two sources close to him said Trump was very angry with Pence, while the second was frustrated and saddened by the US president's actions, according to CNN.

Among the latest Republicans to join Trump's list of backers, Senator Pat Toomey said on Sunday that Trump should resign.

In an interview with the television network "In. B. C: "I think the best course for our country is for the President to resign and leave as soon as possible... I admit this is probably unlikely, but I think it would be the best option. "

Before breaking into Congress, Trump intensified pressure on Pence to push him to block congressional ratification of the results of last November's election, as he sought to remain in power. After confirming that Pence would abide by his official duties, and would not block congressional ratification, Trump's army of supporters in a speech to some of them at the White House, while thousands of them, including members of far-right groups, rallied in Washington to protest the congressional meeting before storming it.

"If Mike Pence does the right thing, we will win the election. He has the absolute right to do so. If he did not, it would be an unfortunate day for our country. "During the chaos in Congress, Trump never called to check on the safety of Pence, who was with his wife Karen and daughter Charlotte at the Capitol. A source close to Pence earlier told CNN that Trump and senior White House officials had made no effort to ensure that Pence and his family were inside the congressional residence. Pelosi announced on Saturday that if Trump did not step down, she had instructed the House Rules Committee to proceed with an impeachment move, based on the 25 amendment. Democrats, who said impeachment could come to the House of Representatives on Monday, hope that threats will intensify pressure on Pence and the government to activate the amendment to oust Trump before his term ends. A copy of the draft articles of impeachment, which members of Congress deliberate among themselves, accused Trump of "inciting violence against the United States government," in an attempt to overturn the outcome of the election he lost to Biden. The articles, which constitute a series of official accusations of mismanagement, were drafted by Democratic representatives, David Chicheln, Ted Liu and Jaime Raskin. The materials were also based on a nearly hour-long call Trump held last week with Georgia's Republican Secretary of State Brad Raffensperger, who asked him to "find" enough votes to invalidate Biden's victory in the state. Two sources familiar with the matter said House Democrats planned to put forward the two articles to demand his removal from office, with a vote to take place next Wednesday.

For his part, Senate Republican Leader Mitch McConnell sent a memo to Republican members, containing a detailed timetable for an impeachment trial. The Council will hold its first working meeting on 19 January and needs the approval of all 100 members to meet earlier (which is unlikely), meaning the trial will not begin until Trump is out of office, according to a source familiar with the document.

Pence pledges to ensure a safe inauguration for Biden... 100 arrested accused of storming Congress

Outgoing U.S. Vice President Donald Trump, Mike Pence, pledged to ensure that the inauguration of President-elect Joe Biden takes place in a secure environment at a time of announcement. B. i) about the arrest of more than 100 in connection with the storming of Congress. Pence's remarks came on Thursday during a visit to Washington by FEMA; To see what measures are being taken for the inauguration ceremony to be held on 20 January.

Pence said in his remarks that "in line with our history and tradition, we will ensure that the inauguration takes place and President-elect Joe Biden is sworn in under secure conditions." B. On Thursday, the office arrested more than a hundred people in connection with last week's congressional blockade and is now investigating individuals likely to threaten the inauguration of President-elect Joe Biden on January 20.

"We are investigating individuals who may be looking to repeat the violence we witnessed last week," Christopher Wray, director of the bureau, said in a special briefing to outgoing Vice President Mike Pence on securing the inauguration ceremony.

"We have identified more than 200 suspects since January 6 only, so we know who you and FBI agents are on their way to find you."

On the same level, the Washington Secret Service announced a list of prohibited contraband during the inauguration and included a number of prohibited materials, indicating that such objects "may cause risks to public safety." Among the prohibitions announced by the Secret Service, "Explosives, laser indicators, flap spray, sprays, ammunition, drones and other drone systems, firearms, flammable liquids, glass, thermal or metal packagings" For its part, Metro announced line service modifications to accommodate the expanded security perimeter that will be in effect for the inauguration ceremony from Friday, January 15 until Thursday, January 21. The company noted that it will "close 13 stations within the security perimeter, with 11 stations closed on Friday and two additional stations closed on Saturday, and continue until the end of service on Thursday." It added that "during this period, trains pass through closed stations without stopping." While supporting law enforcement plans to enhance security, we also maintain essential services for our residents who need work, medical appointments and groceries "

Robert Conte, the acting police chief in Washington, announced that at least 20 thousand members of the National Guard would be deployed to the capital to secure the ceremony. In 2016, some 8 thousand National Guard troops were deployed to secure Trump's inauguration.

Mayor Muriel Boeser urged citizens "not to come to the central commercial downtown area, which extends almost from the east of the Capitol to the Lincoln Memorial and north to Massachusetts Avenue. She also urged potential visitors to stay indoors. " Many parking lots near the Capitol and White House will be closed on Friday, and private parking will be closed in residential buildings near the concert site "Biden's inauguration ceremony is expected to take part in limited numbers of the public due to the coronavirus pandemic and security measures taken after supporters of the outgoing US president, Donald Trump, stormed the congressional building on January 6. All these preparations come against the backdrop of a January 6 break-in at the Washington capital Capitol by supporters reckoned with Trump in a dangerous precedent for American political life, where confrontations took place between security forces and protesters, killing 5 people, including a police officer, and arresting 52 others.

Former US Vice President Mike Pence confirmed that he had not taken any confidential documents with him at the end of his term, and demanded that the Justice Department deal with "transparency" in the investigation of former President Donald Trump. This comes after the FBI released top secret information from Trump's Florida home on August 8 during an investigation into possible violations of three federal laws in the United States. Trump claims the confidential documents were "declassified." The Associated Press asked Pence if he kept any classified information upon leaving office, and replied: "No, as far as I know." Despite the inclusion in a government list of items recovered from Trump's home of material labeled "very confidential," Pence said: "Frankly, I don't want to prejudge it until we know all the facts." Pence again raised the possibility that the investigation would be politically motivated, and called on Justice Secretary Merrick Garland to reveal more details about what led the authorities to raid Trump's home. He said: "The anxiety of millions of Americans will be resolved only in broad daylight. I know that's not normal in an investigation. But this is a precedent from the Ministry of Justice, and I think it deserves transparency. "

Pence was in Iowa on Friday on a two-day trip to the state hosting the Republican caucuses on the presidential election.

This comes after the former Vice President visited other states, while taking steps towards launching a campaign for the next presidential election in 2024. Pence said he would take a decision early next year on whether to run for president, in a move that aides said would be independent of what Trump decides to do, according to AP.

Pence touched on Republican Rep. Liz Cheney's defeat days ago, in front of a contest she supported Trump in the Wyoming Republican primary. Cheney is considered to be one of the former President's most enemies, calling him a "very serious threat and danger to our Republic", and angered him even more by her role as Vice President of a Parliamentary Commission of Inquiry in the events of 6 January 2021 that saw supporters of Trump storm the Capitol, in an effort to prevent lawmakers from ratifying Joe Biden's election as President of the United States. Pence, who was targeted during the Capitol break-in, chanted supporters of Trump at the time, calling for his hanging, considered that "the people of Wyoming gave their opinion," adding: "I accept their judgment on what kind of representation they wanted in the Capitol." He noted that he had "great respect" for Liz Cheney's father, former Vice President Dick Ch, and continued: But I've been disappointed with the partisan tone of Committee 6 January since early. "

Aides to Pence stated that the Committee had contacted his legal team months earlier, to determine his willingness to testify before it.

Pence said that he would give "due consideration" to cooperation with the Committee, but that "other than my concerns about the partisan nature of the Committee 6 January, there are deep constitutional issues to be taken into account. no Vice-President has been called to testify before Congress in the United States ".

Despite his disagreement with Trump after the events of January 6, Pence was careful not to alienate Republicans who supported the former president, but could be looking for another candidate in the 2024 election.

Republicans were urged to stop attacking the FBI, about the raid on Trump's home. Pence said Wednesday: "The Republican Party is the party of law and order... These attacks must depend on the Office. "

Former US Vice President Mike Pence continued his "opposition" directions to former President Donald Trump with a new statement that could hint at a future Republican contest between the two men. Former Vice President Mike Pence said he would consider testifying before the House "6 January" committee if requested, which Trump does not recognize, because it investigates his involvement in the riots by his supporters on Capitol Hill. According to ABC, Pence said: "If there is an invitation to participate, I will keep it in mind." Pence's answer was a new "clash" with his former chairman, Donald Trump, who repeatedly criticized the work of the 6 January Commission as politically motivated. According to ABC, for months, the Commission's investigators have been communicating privately with Pence's lawyers about securing his testimony in the events of the Capitol break-in.

Mike Pence was described as a "hero of the hour"; The man who stood his ground in the face of Donald Trump's "coup" plot, saved America from a violent movement.

However, Pence was not present among witnesses, reporters, members of Congress, women, young citizens and members of the parliamentary committee at a hearing on Thursday on the January 6, 2020, Capitol attack.

Pence was 500 miles from Washington, specifically in Ohio, to promote "American dominance of energy."

The two events lead in the same direction: Pence 2024, a presidential campaign that at one time was unlikely, but which sheds light on the former vice president's complex relationship with Trump, according to the British newspaper The Guardian.

"Amicable separation." Mike Pence reveals his relationship with Trump

Pence has already hinted at his presidential candidacy, from being founded by Advansing American Freedom, to tours of the battlegrounds of the Republican primary. But nothing a 63-year-old would say in an early election campaign can be as decisive as the three-hour session that took place in his absence on Thursday, in front of millions of viewers.

Contrary to what Trump supporters wanted, the Parliamentary Commission of Inquiry into the Capitol Events praised Pence, and did not comment on the gallows, where she spoke of a man who put his allegiance to the country ahead of Trump, something Republican voters who wanted to move forward away from the former president could use. But the hearing could also be a major impediment for Pence between the Trump voter base, which, in her view, is hardening and regards the former Vice President as a "traitor." The third plenary hearing of the Parliamentary Committee addressed Trump's attempts to pressure Pence to overturn his defeat in the 2020 election; She heard testimony that Trump had been repeatedly told that Pence lacked constitutional and legal authority to meet his demands.

Resistance and courage

Penny Thompson, Chairman of the Committee, began the hearing with a remark: "Mike Pence said no. Resist pressure. He knew it was illegal. He knew it was wrong. We are fortunate to have Mr. Pence's courage on 6 January. Our democracy came very close to a catastrophe, and that courage put it in tremendous danger".

While Vice Chairman Liz Cheney, who could run against Pence in 2024, said: "Pence understood that his swearing-in was more important than his loyalty to Donald Trump. He performed his duty. President Trump has categorically not done so".

The committee heard how Trump stuck to the "ridiculous" plan of conservative law professor John Eastman, and launched a public and private pressure campaign on Pence days before he chaired the Congressional Committee to certify Joe Biden's election victory.

The Committee noted that a confidential informant had informed the FBI that the right-wing group "Proud Boys" would have killed Pence if they had had the opportunity.

Made in United States
North Haven, CT
13 November 2022

26666465R00024